Running a Support Group

---*for*---

Separated, Divorced

---&---

Remarried Catholics
(S.D.R.C.)

---*by*---

Rev. William Murphy, S.A. & Diana Oddo

Buckley Publications
Chicago, Illinois

RUNNING A SUPPORT GROUP
For Separated, Divorced & Remarried Catholics

By Rev. William Murphy, S.A. and Diana Oddo

All rights reserved. No part of this publication may be reproduced or transmitted in any form or by any means, electronic or mechanical, including photocopying and recording, or by any information storage and retrieval system, without permission in writing from Buckley Publications, Inc.

Copyright ©1987: Buckley Publications, Inc.
4848 N. Clark Street
Chicago, Illinois 60640
312-271-0202

ISBN No. 0-915388-27-8

Library of Congress Catalog No. 87-071987

Printed in the United States of America

CONTENTS

A PERSONAL WORD 1

CHAPTER I
HISTORICAL PERSPECTIVE OF THE
SEPARATED DIVORCED MINISTRY 3

CHAPTER II
BASIC GOALS FOR SUPPORT GROUPS 9

CHAPTER III
GROUPS 15

CHAPTER IV
PROGRAMS 29

CHAPTER V
LEADERSHIP 55

CHAPTER VI
HOW TO PUBLICIZE YOUR GROUP 65

CHAPTER VII
RESOURCES 71

ACKNOWLEDGMENTS

We sincerely appreciate the willingness of others to allow us to include samples of their material for the divorced, separated and remarried in this book. The following excerpts are included with these permissions. Further reproduction is prohibited without permission.

From REBUILDING: WHEN YOUR RELATIONSHIP ENDS, ©1981 by Bruce Fisher, Impact Publishers, Inc., P.O. Box 1094, San Luis Obispo, California 93406, pp. 34-35

From LINK PROGRAM, Diocese of Buffalo, Family Life Office, 795 Main Street, Buffalo, New York, 14203, pp. 31-34

From DIVORCE PROGRAM, by Br. James Greteman and Leon Haverkamp, Office of Catholic Charities, P.O. Box 1366, Salina, Kansas 67402, pp. 35-37

From DIVORCE AND BEYOND, by Br. James Greteman and Leon Haverkamp, Buckley Publications, 4848 N. Clark Street, Chicago, Illinois 60640, pp. 37-39

From MOVING ON AFTER DIVORCE; GETTING UNSTUCK, by LeRoy Spaniol and Paul Lannan, Paulist Press, 997 MacArthur Boulevard, Mahwah, New Jersey 07430, pp 39-40

From COPING WITH STRESS, HANDLING STRESS, FORMING A CONSCIENCE, FACING THE HOLIDAY, DEALING WITH EMOTIONS: CHILDREN, etc., by Dorothy J. Levesque, Director, Diocese of Providence, Ministry with Separated, Divorced, Remarried and Widowed Persons, One Cathedral Square, Providence, Rhode Island 02903, pp. 41-45, 59-60, 80-84

From STEPS TO WHOLENESS, Archdiocese of St. Louis, ARISE Ministry, 4140 Lindell Boulevard, St. Louis, Missouri 63108, pp. 45-47

From STEPS TO RECOVERY, by John F. Redman and Peggy Kenna Redman, 723 W. Curry, Chandler, Arizona 95224, pp. 47-48

From HOPE HOLDS ON, by Joanna Dunn and Rev. Anton Braun, O.F.M., Alverna Center, 8140 Spring Mill Road, Indianapolis, Indiana 46260, pp. 49-52

FR. BILL MURPHY

A PERSONAL WORD

Eight years ago when I began this ministry to the Separated, Divorced, Remarried and Widowed, little did I think that I would be so much involved with so many hurting people who have gone through the trauma of a separation.

A young woman of about thirty came into my office crying because she did not know where to turn for help. She had no money, she was away from her many friends for she had lived over a thousand miles away for most of her married life, she had no job, and she had a five year old daughter who needed attention.

I soon realized that there were no groups in the area who would be able to support her in her misery. The local school administrator told me that sixty percent of the children in the school came from single family homes. Something had to be done, so I started my first group at the Chapel of Our Saviour in Brockton, Mass. This one group led me to form other groups so that before I left the south shore of Boston, I had many mini-groups, all under the direction of the Chapel to which I was assigned.

Four years ago, I was transferred back to Graymoor to enter the retirement community of our Society. I was asked to help out with the separated, divorced and remarried people who were coming to Graymoor for help. This also led me to form other groups who would be a support to these hurting people.

During these eight years I never found a person who entered marriage with the intention of getting a divorce later on in life. But I knew that something had to be done to help those who were separated, divorced or widowed. I was aware that there was no one who could help these people more than those who had undergone the trauma of a separation.

The groups that I formed are made up of people who had been there, people who had gone through the loneliness, the guilt, the bitterness, and the loss so that they could help others who were going through what they themselves had already gone through.

But there was one more problem. Each group that was formed needed direction as to how to start, maintain and publicize a group. It seemed that each time I started a new group I would have to go over the same things time and time again. So--the reason for such a manual as this came to mind, not only for my own groups, but also for others who are in the same situation.

I was happy to have the person who is at present my executive coordinator of Graymoor SDRC to help me with this manual. Together we have been forming groups during the past years and together we have put this manual together to help others.

If we can help others who are forming groups, we are happy to do so.

I
HISTORICAL PERSPECTIVE OF THE SEPARATED DIVORCED MINISTRY

If you fail to plan, you will plan to fail.

When, in 1972, a few separated and divorced Catholics approached the late Father Jim Young at the Paulist Center in Boston to ask what the Church could do for them, he had no idea that fifteen years later there would be a widespread ministry to separated and divorced Catholics across the United States, Canada and Mexico. Today, there are more than one thousand support groups of separated and divorced across the North American continent. Fr. Young also could not have envisioned the growth of the organization called the North American Conference of Separated and Divorced Catholics (NACSDC). NACSDC holds its annual conference at Notre Dame University in Indiana and operates through Regional Conferences organized according to the 13 Ecclesiastical Regions in the United States and 4 in Canada.

People like Jim Young and Paula Ripple, past director of NACSDC, have done more for this ministry than anyone will ever know. Together with all those who had ministered to the separated and divorced—as well as the separated and divorced themselves—they have made this unique ministry what it is today: a healing ministry within a compassionate Church, from which many separated and divorced persons have benefited. Many alienated persons have found their way back to the Church through this ministry.

In addition to NACSDC, three other national organizations have contributed to the development of the ministry to divorced, separated and remarried Catholics. The Canon Law Society of America (CLSA), through the marriage tribunal in each diocese, has helped thousands of divorced Catholics obtain a declaration of nullity (or annulment) which has allowed them to remarry in a Catholic ceremony. The National Association of Catholic Diocesan Family Life Ministers (NACDFLM) encourages and supports local family life offices in each diocese which conduct a variety of programs for separated, divorced and remarried Catholics. Catholic Charities U.S.A., through diocesan Catholic Charities or Catholic Family Services, also provides a wide range of services to individuals during separation, divorce and remarriage.

The key to ministry to separated, divorced and remarried Catholics, however, has from the very beginning been found in local support groups. These groups have been organized in various ways. Some were formed due to the efforts of a national organization, many were developed by a local diocese or parish, and a large number were organized at the initiative of Catholic lay people going through separation, divorce or remarriage themselves.

Our own Graymoor Affiliates is a good example. In June 1974, a conference entitled "The Christian Churches and Divorce" was held at the Graymoor Friary in New York State. At the end of the conference, a panel of divorced Catholics presented a constructive view of their spiritual needs. In response, the Graymoor Christian Unity Center conducted a retreat that year for divorced Catholics. As a result of this retreat, the first separated, divorced and remarried Catholic (SDRC) group in the area was founded. Organized into a series of neighborhood support groups, the "Graymoor Affiliates" numbered 12 mini-groups with a membership of almost 1000 members by 1987.

Similar examples are possible from across the continent. Experience has shown that SDRC support groups are both needed and popular by those they seek to serve. Running such groups is not difficult. In many ways, they run themselves.

This book merely seeks to provide some simple directions for those interested in beginning or operating a support group for separated, divorced and remarried Catholics. It provides examples of what has worked for our group and others around the country. It lists resources that have proved useful and warns of difficulties to be anticipated.

Both Fr. Murphy and I hope and pray that our observations are useful to you.

Diana Oddo
Executive Coordinator
Graymoor Associates

II
BASIC GOALS FOR SUPPORT GROUPS

A well laid plan is always very profitable.

1. TO DEVELOP A POSITIVE CHRISTIAN LIFE STYLE OF SEPARATED, DIVORCED OR REMARRIED CATHOLIC

The support groups which we have in mind in this manual is based on the laws of the Roman Catholic Church. To develop ideals and means to assist each person who comes to us for help, we affirm that we must follow not only the dogmatic teachings of the Catholic Church, but also we follow the laws of the magisterium, which is the Holy Father and the Bishops of the Church, who make decisions as to morality.

To develop a positive Christian Life Style such as to go to Church, to try to live by the Gospel, to make an earnest effort to live a life according to the ten commandments, to love God and our neighbor as we love ourselves.

Even though we welcome others not of the Catholic faith to participate and join our support groups, we state that we must follow the laws of the Catholic Church in all that we do in our support groups.

The remarried people who come to our groups should come with the understanding that we will assist them, not only in their problems of the blended families, social problems, communication problems, but always with the philosophy that marriage is inviolable, and that marriage is a community of love between two persons.

2. TO CULTIVATE IN OURSELVES A SENSE OF MINISTRY TO ONE ANOTHER AS OUR CHRISTIAN VOCATION

The support group gains its help from a person who has been through a separation or a divorce to assist those who are just beginning to go through the process of a separation.

It is a proven fact that some of the best lessons can be learned from a separation or divorce can be learned from others who have been there, who have become whole persons and developed a sense of true values within their own lives and thus will be able to assist those who are going through the separation a short time before.

The purpose of the support group is to help others to learn more about their prayer life, their working through problems of becoming a whole person and finally how to play so that the newly separated person will be able to become a whole person once again.

It is better to give than receive and many people in the support groups are able to give to others, and can follow the Divine Commandment to love and support one another.

3. TO PROVIDE A SPIRITUAL GUIDANCE FOR THOSE WHOSE MARRIAGES ARE UNABLE TO CONFORM TO CHURCH LAW

Pope John Paul II has said that every person who is baptized is a member of the Catholic Church. He enjoins all bishops and priests to assist each person pastorally who is not able to participate in the full life of the Church.

The goal of each support group is to assist these people and make them feel that they are members of the Catholic Church, should be treated as a human being, to be made to feel at home by the attendance at the Sacred Liturgy, to participate in the prayer life of the Church and to assist them as other human beings in all their problems of life.

To provide means whereby their former marriages can be annulled, if possible, through an annulment in the Tribunal of their diocese in the Catholic Church.

To assist in remarriage groups so that those people who are remarried can find solace, comfort and support in the many problems that stem from their remarriage.

4. TO PROMOTE AN UNDERSTANDING OF THE NEEDS OF SEPARATED, DIVORCED AND REMARRIED CATHOLICS IN THE CHURCH

It is not uncommon that many people who call themselves Catholics do not understand or comprehend the needs of the separated, divorced or remarried Catholics. It is the obligation of the support groups to bring about through information, by dialogue, by meetings, even by bringing pressure on those who do not understand what the Catholic Church teaches concerning the position of the separated people. <ins>SETTING GOALS FOR THE GROUP</ins>

To bring to the attention of the local Bishop, the Chancery Office, the Pastor and the Parish Council that each one of us has an obligation to be a Christian to our fellow man and that each one of us should be considerate and helpful to our separated and divorced people.

To promote a better understanding of the great trauma that a separated, divorced or remarried person goes through in such a separation to all those people in the community.

To use the media such as the press, radio, TV and other forms of dissemination of information to the community to bring to the attention of difficulties of each separated, divorced or remarried person.

It should be mentioned that it is NOT NECESSARY FOR THE CORE GROUP TO DEVELOP BY-LAWS before starting a group. The most important thing is to set goals for the group, namely to be of service and help hurting people of the separated, divorced and remarried community.

III
GROUPS

As you think so you act, therefore think and plan your future life

A. DEFINITION OF A SUPPORT GROUP

Individuals in a similar state of life, with similar problems trying to help each other overcome these problems. Support groups provide mutual healing, temporary harbors for persons whose lives are adrift due to the trauma of separation and divorce. An SDRC support group is a spiritually based self help group for those who have experienced loss and/or rejection through divorce, or separation. SDRC is a place where you can work through the grieving process of divorce. Some may work through their process quickly, others may need more time. Everyone is accepted as they are, and given spiritual, emotional and social support. Some take what they need and return to the mainstream, others assume leadership roles or commit themselves to the ministry. Confidentiality is emphasized at all meetings "what you hear here, stays here."

A support group is based in a local area. Usually it is within the confines of a parish or a group of parishes that join together to help each person in the group. It is necessary for each person in the support group to understand that the support group is for the benefit of the individual rather than for the group to be a continuing social or other type of group.

It is limited to just the separated, divorced people of the area. The reason for this is that the separated and divorced people have to go through the grieving process for it is a type of grieving that is peculiar to their particular trauma. Each person has to go through this process in his or her own time, but the support group will help the person to overcome the difficulties of their state in life as a single person.

The idea of a support group is that it will help people who are primarily in the beginnings of the grieving process. Others, after they have gone through the grieving process may still attend to help the beginners, to have their own socials, to have their own spiritual exercises, but it should always be the beginners in the group that need the most attention and which the Church wants to help in pastoral manner.

It is better for the widows to have their own group for the grieving process although somewhat the same as the divorced person, but it is much different for this group. There is seldom any bitterness towards their former spouse and their former life. Their grieving takes on the loneliness, the bitterness towards God for taking their former spouse, their guilt for not doing enough for the former spouses in life.

B. PURPOSE

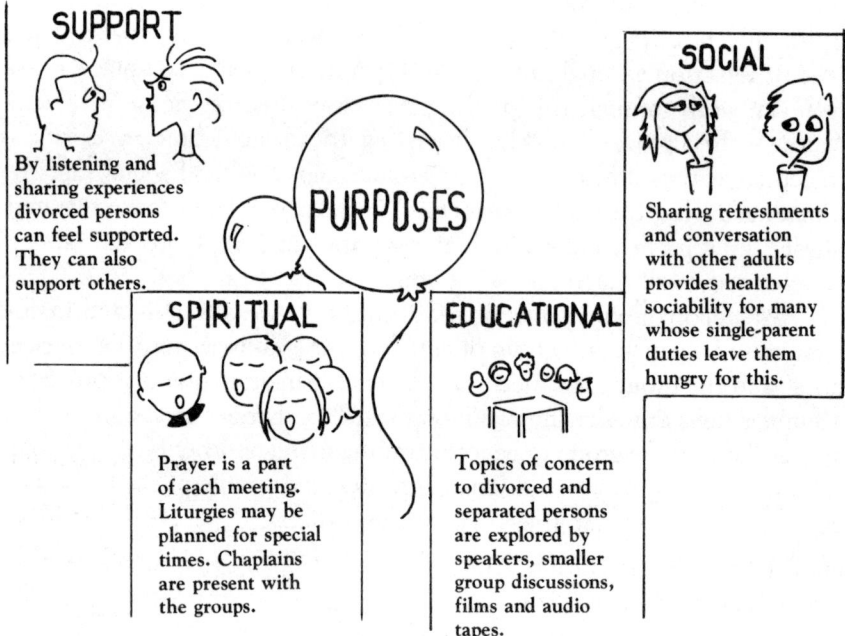

C. HOW TO START A SUPPORT GROUP

There are probably as many variations as to how to start a group as there are groups. The following are some organizational steps that all groups must take.

1. Someone has to WANT to start a group or see a NEED for it.

2. You need to contact a Parish Priest for support. (This contact could also be with a Sister or Deacon). In order for a group to continue to grow the support and physical presences of a religious is important. This has been found true throughout the Ministry.

3. You need a Core Group of people who are willing to commit themselves for at least one year. In keeping with scripture the number twelve represents the disciples. Something to think about. Aren't we all disciples? (Could be two, four, or six). **COMMITMENT**

4. The Core Group meets for six weeks to two months for the purpose of, learning about each other, forming a community, learning about what groups are, how to facilitate groups, how to plan for the group, visit other existing groups if possible.

5. Next the Core Group decides how they want to present SDRC into the Parish.

a.) Hold a one day Parish Day or Night, providing talks on pertinent topics as Recovery Process, Grieving Process, Annulments, Church's laws regarding the Separated and Divorced. **ORGANIZATION**

-or-

b.) Set up a regular scheduled meeting/rap session/lecture. Subsequent meetings should be scheduled at least twice a month. (Please note: Once a time, date, and place is established try not to change it. Members need the security to know there is a regular meeting).

6. Publicize. At least one month prior to Parish Day/Regular meeting, advertisements should be placed in area Church bulletins, local papers, Pennysaver, Post Office, Library, Supermarkets, local radio station. You may even want to speak at Masses two weeks prior to your meeting. **PUBLICIZE**

Here is a sample step by step outline:

6 WEEKS BEFORE

Contact two others to help plan.
Visit the Pastor and explain the Support Group purpose.
Request use of a Parish Meeting Room.

5 WEEKS BEFORE

Decide a topic for the first meeting.
Engage a speaker or arrange for audio-visuals.
Write an article about the Meeting. Include time, date, topic, speaker.

4 WEEKS BEFORE

Send article to: Parish bulletins in the area.
Local Newspapers
Family Life Office
Local radio stations

3 WEEKS BEFORE

Design posters about the Support Group Meeting.
Request placement of them in stores and shopping centers.

2 WEEKS BEFORE

Make phone calls to "pass the word on" to
Local Parish Priest
School Principals
Religious Education Staff
Send a SECOND article to Parish bulletin, local paper, Family Life Office, Local radio station.

1 WEEK BEFORE

Buy or make Name Tags.
Make signs for directions to meeting room.
Check room arrangements
Divide responsibility for night of the meeting among Core Group.
Finalize agenda for first meeting.

BEFORE THE 1st MEETING

Arrive 30 minutes early
Plug in coffee and hot water
Set up room comfortably
Bring name tags and marking pens
Greet participants as they arrive

Groups

Newly formed Groups generally go through five stages or phases of transition.

1. POLITE STAGE—When you first start everyone is polite. This might also be called the Orientation Phase.
2. GROUP DISORGANIZATION STAGE—There appears to be a lot of rambling, joking, if this continues the group will fall apart.
3. NEGATIVE/AGGRESSIVE STAGE—Group may go through transition, may have to deal with conflicts, resistance, struggle for control (who's in charge here?) This is where the group starts integrating. "Have Faith" stage.
4. INTERPERSONAL STAGE—or working stage. Cohesion starts to take place, productive work results. The group starts to function as a group. The group starts to relax, there's less tension.
5. CREATIVE ENCOUNTER STAGE—"What can we do." How can we expand the group. There's follow up, evaluation.

D. HOW TO RUN A GROUP

Again there are many models of how to run a group. PLANNING is most important. The following is a sample worksheet of an SDRC meeting. You might find something such as this helpful in planning meetings.

PLANNING WORKSHOP WORKSHEET
SDRC MEETING OUTLINE

(SAMPLE)

PROGRAM: _____ DATE: _____

PRE OPENING: REMEMBER: _____

- Prepare meeting place
- Give out name tags
- Activities for early arrivals
- Welcome newcomers
- Library set up
- Well charts

TIME: _____

LEADER: _____

OPENING: REMEMBER: _____

- Opening prayer/ceremony
- Announcements
- Old business
- New business

TIME: _____

LEADER: _____

PROGRAM FEATURE: REMEMBER: _____

- Teaching
- Demonstration
- Guest speaker

TIME: _____

LEADER: _____

SOCIAL BREAK:

- Coffee/refreshments
- Contests, 50/50 drawings

TIME: _____

LEADER: _____

REMEMBER: _____
_____
_____

GROUP DISCUSSIONS:

- Assign leaders
- Select group spokesperson
- Discuss ideas related to program

TIME: _____

LEADER: _____

REMEMBER: _____
_____
_____

INTERGROUP ACTIVITIES:

- Reports/decisions on coming events
- demonstrations

TIME: _____

LEADER: _____

REMEMBER: _____
_____
_____

CLOSING:

- Announcements
- Recognition, awards
- Spiritual Moderators input
- Closing prayer, ceremony

TIME: _____

LEADER: _____

REMEMBER: _____
_____
_____

AFTER MEETING:

- Leaders brief evaluation of meeting, check details for next meeting
- Clean up

REMEMBER: _____
_____
_____

Every meeting should open and close with a prayer, song, or reflection. Announcements should be kept SHORT. (You may want to prepare a monthly calendar of events as a handout.) Format of meetings will vary. If there are two meetings a month, one meeting might host a guest speaker such as a priest talking on annulments, or a local attorney speaking on legal aspects.

You may choose to have just a Sharing Session or Rap Session, consisting of small groups (6-8) discussing various topics.

It may be necessary to meet with your Core Group at least one time during the month either prior to regular meetings or just after regular meetings for the purpose of feedback. Were there any breakdowns? Was everyone on task? What changes need to be made for the next meeting. You may choose to meet right after a meeting for a few minutes just to evaluate that evenings program. REMEMBER! Change is O.K.

It is important to remember the Core group/Support group relationship. Core group members MUST MINGLE at meetings not to show a click. This also holds true for social events. Fifty percent (50%) do not come back, maybe because they did not feel WELCOME.

Try to greet members at the door, follow up with a phone call. Be sensitive to members, sensitive to people sitting out in the car in the parking lot. You may want to use different colored name tags for New members.

You can expect changes in attendance from members. Regulars will come consistently. Others will attend sporadically. And some will come only once. Usually there is high anxiety at meetings.

__LISTEN__

Shifting of chairs, talkativeness, walking around, giggling. Some members may withdraw, some will ask questions without listening to answers. It is important to remember during meetings to make sure there is a sharing on the topic. Listening to others' ideas.

Other suggestions that have proved successful are:

- Have a few members positioned in the parking lot prior to the meeting. We have found some new members never made it out of the car.

- Have parking lot, entrance walls WELL SIGNED, as to how to get to the meeting room.

Groups

- Set up a "buddy system" at meetings, newcomers with one color name tags, regular members with another. Newcomers committee responsible for newcomers at meetings, sitting with them, introducing them to other members, "stick by their side" for that night.

- Set up a phone committee to call newcomers two days after the meeting just to say "Hi."

- Follow up call to newcomers before next meeting. "Looking forward to seeing you there."

It can not be emphasized enough how important it is to take much time in planning for the newcomers. The two most important committees are the Newcomers Committee and Welcoming Committee. Remember the old phrase about "First Impressions."

Having a separate rap group for newcomers attending the meeting for the first time is also important. One or two of the members who are moving along the grieving process would make good group facilitators for the newcomers. They are much closer to the raw feelings than someone way down the road.

There is another important aspect of a meeting that should be mentioned. It has been found that some type of closure of a meeting is necessary. Members come to meetings feeling very alone and isolated. The meeting, the topic and interchange with other members, can provide a stimulation and need for more dialogue. We have found sharing a cup of coffee and pie at the local diner or a glass of wine or soda at the local Pub, after a meeting allows a way for our members to bring closure to the evening.

Possible types of Chairpersons needed. All of these positions will vary with size and structure of the group.

1. *Core Leader/Coordinator:* acts as a representative of the group when in contact with the church/priest, Spiritual Moderator, potential member, member or newcomer, etc. Plans and coordinates the activities of the group. Follows up by letter, phone or in person to see that all the activities of the group as planned are carried out. Delegate or asks for volunteers for jobs if necessary. Actively "Listens" to members on a spiritual, moral, social and intellectual level. Keeps informed of changes within the Ministry and pass it along to membership. Ultimately, the leaders job is to GET THE JOB DONE.

2. *Secretary:* keeps minutes of the meeting. Possibly sends birthday cards to members. Sends "Thank You's" to guest speakers. Assist the leaders in sending correspondence as needed.

3. *Treasurer:* Collect dues and coffee money donated. Quarterly check with the coordinator and the mini group members whether the dues and coffee monies are adequate to cover the cost of expenses. Records all intake. Gives cash for any disbursements receipts are submitted for. Keeps running balance and report to the group at each meeting.

4. *Welcoming Committee:* Should arrive at least ½ hour before meeting. Greet newcomers as they arrive, make introductions, escort to Newcomers group, give name tag and any handouts that might be useful. Keep a list of newcomers and members at each meeting. Committee makes sure everyone is networking before the meeting starts, and that there is no newcomer left alone or no member standing in a corner by themselves.

5. *Publicity:* Attend meetings to pick up information for news releases or other publicity. Prepare and distribute news releases.

6. *Social Coordinator:* Responsible to survey, organize, and plan social functions for group. Especially being aware of low cost or no cost events. Organizing carpools if necessary. Confer with group leaders of possible social events for group.

7. *Hospitality Committee:* Responsible for setting up Coffee, tea, cookies or cakes. Request from members donations of cakes or cookies for next meeting. Have coffee ready at beginning of meeting. This may mean being there at least ½ hour before. Purchase supplies as needed. Responsible for clean up of Coffee area.

Other types of Chairpersons: Program coordinator, Librarian.

GENERAL GROUND RULES FOR SMALL GROUPS

1. This is not a therapy group. We are here to share our own feelings and experiences.
2. Respect and maintain the confidentiality of the group.
3. Our goal is to accept people, and to avoid making judgments.
4. Give supportive attention to any person who is speaking.
5. Avoid interrupting. If we do break in, return the conversation to the person who was speaking.
6. Side conversations are not allowed.
7. We each share the responsibility for making this group work.
8. We each have the opportunity for equal air time or the right to remain silent.
9. We try not to discuss persons who are not present.
10. We try not to give or take advice.
11. We have the right to ask questions and the right to refuse to answer.

The group may not be what you are looking for, but give it more than one try before deciding.

IV
PROGRAMS

**Link
Divorce and Beyond
and
Steps to Wholeness**

Knowing just who you are is one of the greatest gems of life. Study to know just who you are.

There are many published programs that we have found helpful.

We first incorporated the levels of the LINK program out of the Diocese of Buffalo, to get a bases of where our members were at in the grieving process. The following is a sample of the Link program. For more information you can contact the Buffalo Diocesan Representative, Joan Meier, 1246 89th Street, Niagara Falls, New York 14304.

WHAT IS LINK?

LINK is an organization of lay ministers reaching out to separated and divorced people who need:

- to be in touch with self
- to re-discover a sense of personal belonging to family and Church,

and

- to re-root relationships within self, with God, family, and Church.

The spiritual dimension of this group comes from the God within each of us. We minister to each other by caring, giving and sharing. In helping others, we best help ourselves.

LINK offers opportunities to grow through various workshops, retreats, family activities, social events and the LEVELS PROGRAM.

Our main program consists of the following three levels:

Level I

—for those separated or divorced in the initial grieving stages, generally less than 2 years.

—orientation/registration night followed by an 8 week program with discussion group format, meeting every other week.

Level II

—for those beyond level I and in the rebuilding stage.

—orientation/registration night followed by a 6 week program with discussion group format, meeting every 3 weeks.

Level III

—for those beyond the 1st and 2nd levels who wish to maintain LINK ties.

—a large group meeting held four times a year and open to people in *all levels*.

—presentation by a resource person on topics relative to this level followed by small group discussion. These groups will be formed according to the individual's level.

LEVEL I

1. Do you feel the need to talk about what happened in your marriage?
2. Do you feel that your ex-spouse has the biggest responsibility for the break-up of your marriage?
3. Do you find it hard to deal with the memories both good and bad?
4. Does it hurt all over?
5. Do you feel empty—like someone cut off a part of you?
6. Do you feel like your feelings are drowning you?
7. Do you have wild fluctuations in mood—"Five minutes ago I was crying and now I am laughing"?
8. Do you feel trapped—can't go back—can't go forward?
9. Does your mind wander so much that you are unable to focus on one thing?
10. Do you feel like you are going crazy?

11. Do you have feelings of guilt?
12. Do you feel like you're filled with anger?
13. Does your anger flare up frequently at seemingly little things?
14. Do tears come often for seemingly no reason?
15. Are you lonely but afraid to reach out to others?

YOU PROBABLY NEED THE SUPPORT OF PEOPLE IN "LEVEL I"!!!

LEVEL II

1. Do you want to work to improve your self concept?
2. Are you willing to accept responsibility for your part in the breakup of your marriage without feeling guilty?
3. Are you ready to begin building new, meaningful relationships, both male and female?
4. Are you ready to find new way of communicating and relating to parents, children, friends and co-workers?
5. Are you willing to look at how your attitudes from the past contributed to the break-up of your marriage—influences of parents and significant others?
6. Are you willing to see life as a journey and yourself on the road?
7. Are you ready to begin to love yourself?
8. Are you ready to look at new and different definitions of love?
9. Are you ready to investigate how you feel about yourself as a woman/man?
10. Are you ready to begin learning how to trust again?
11. Are you willing to begin taking risks by sharing your true feelings?
12. Are you ready to re-look at your attitudes and values regarding sex?

13. Are you willing to look at ways to develop a complete and satisfying life for yourself as a "single"?
14. Are you ready to make a commitment to yourself to change your life for the better?

THEN YOU PROBABLY ARE READY TO START *"LEVEL II"*

Bruce Fisher publishes "Rebuilding, When Your Relationship Ends," which is based on the Rebuilding Blocks. This book and program can be broken down into a sixteen week program.

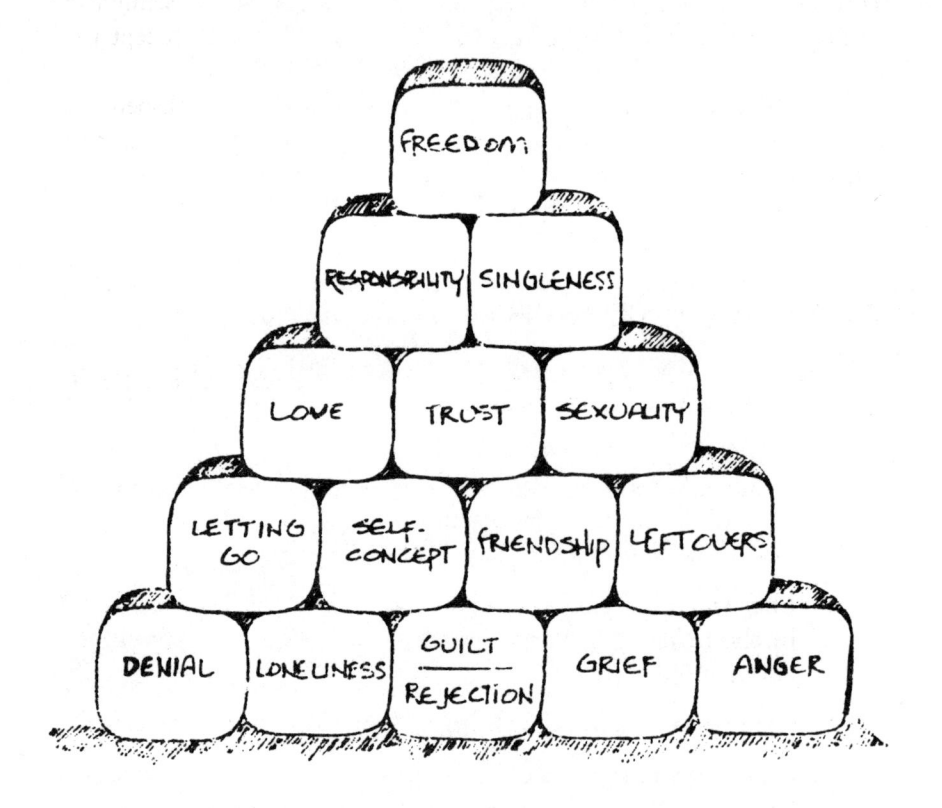

```
                    FREEDOM

            RESPONSIBILITY   SINGLENESS

         LOVE      TRUST      SEXUALITY

   LETTING   SELF-     FRIENDSHIP   LEFTOVERS
     GO      CONCEPT

                    GUILT
  DENIAL  LONELINESS  ———     GRIEF    ANGER
                   REJECTION
```

DENIAL: "IT'LL NEVER HAPPEN TO ME"

None of us plans to be divorced. In our marriage vows, we promised commitment "till death us do part." Divorce only happened to others, but would never happen to us!

But divorce does happen for some of us. We discover that our love-relationship is ending, but we don't want anyone to know. We are afraid to admit failure, and we fear rejection by our friends. Throughout our lives, from the news media, church sermons, and teachers at school, we have been taught that divorce is wrong and destructive. It may feel as though a big "D" suddenly appears on one's forehead. We want to deny that divorce is part of our lives.

Nona talked hesitantly about taking the 10-week seminar, and finally was able to describe her hesitation. "If I took the divorce seminar, it would mean that my marriage is over, and I don't want to accept that yet."

Brother James Greteman and Leon Haverkamp have published "Divorce Program." This program has structured discussion sheets starting with crisis, transition, and overload and ending with love and marriage. The following is an excerpt from this program.

SIX EXPERIENCES OF DIVORCE

These six experiences of divorce may overlap and come in different order.

1. EMOTIONAL DIVORCE begins when the spouses withhold emotion from their relationship. It generally begins before separation and continues for some time afterward.

2. LEGAL DIVORCE occurs when the final decree is handed down by the judge.

3. ECONOMIC DIVORCE occurs when the individuals set up separate housekeeping and separate residences are established.

4. CO-PARENTAL DIVORCE is the separating of mothering and fathering roles that is made necessary when separate residences are established.

5. COMMUNITY DIVORCE involves the loosening of bonds with some old friends and acquaintances, and the beginning of new ones.

6. PSYCHIC DIVORCE deals with individual autonomy. Persons who have lived together for years must separate their identities when they divorce.

... Bohannan

STARTING OVER INCLUDES THREE SUB-STAGES

A) Shock and denial.

B) Transition (disorganization, depression, unmanageable restlessness).

C) Recovery, which usually takes three to five years to complete.

... Weiss

BRIEF PROCESS OF DIVORCE

1. DENIAL first occurs during the emotional divorce. The divorcing person does not want to recognize the signs of decay of the relationship.

2. When at least one person realizes something is wrong, feelings of *LOSS* and *DEPRESSION* occur. If divorce is not discussed as a possibility, feelings of isolation are intensified. It can be helpful for the person to verbalize the feelings of fear at the impending loss of a spouse, a marriage, and a way of life.

3. *ANGER* and *AMBIVALENCE* become prominent in the stage of haggling over property, custody, and visitation rights. One person may call the other spouse to discuss details of property settlement and argue on the telephone for a long time, for example. The positive emotional bonds are not broken immediately, but seem to require being transformed first into negative ones.

For more information contact:

Catholic Charities
P O Box 1366
Salina, Kansas 67402

Brother James Greteman and Leon Haverkamp also have published "Divorce and Beyond." (Buckley Publications, Inc., Chicago, Ill.) This program is designed for people who are already divorced or have filed for divorce. The program is designed for an eight week session. The eight sessions consist of Process of Divorce, Self-image, Stress, Anger, More on Anger, Blame and Guilt, Loneliness, Pathways to Growth. The books are published in paperback format, and consist of a Participants book and Facilitators book. The following is an excerpt from the Participants book.

1) THE DEATH OF THE RELATIONSHIP

This happens in two ways. In about ten percent of the cases, it is a "sudden death"—for example, when one spouse comes home one night and announces that he or she is leaving. However, in most cases, it is a "lingering death" that extends over months or even years. The relationship dies long before the couple decide to file for a divorce.

```
              [HIGH C]
DEATH OF THE      /\          LIFE
RELATIONSHIP     /  \      RE    CONTINUES
A==========B   /    \    GA    E
  MARRIAGE           \  IN   /
     TO               \ IN  /
  SEPARATION           \ G /
                        \ /BALANCE
              [LOW C]||||||||||||||||| D
                   MOURNING PERIOD
```

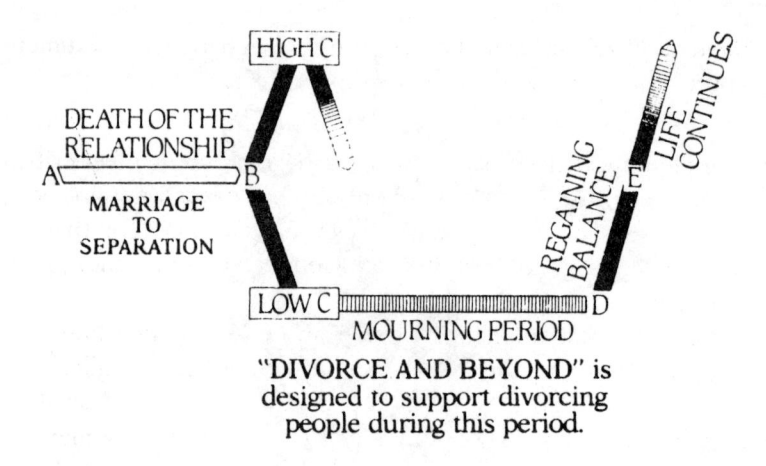

"DIVORCE AND BEYOND" is
designed to support divorcing
people during this period.

Marriages wind up in divorce courts for widely different reasons. However, one common theme is the couples' difficulty in communicating to each other what they expected the marriage relationship to provide for themselves and their partners.

It is impossible to sum up the complex relationships between two human beings who live intimately with each other. Therefore we will only touch on some basic needs that spouses expect their marriage to fulfill.

The first basic need is survival: money for food, shelter, clothing. Because it is obvious, couples seldom have problems *communicating* this need (what they *do* is another matter). Less understood, and often very difficult to communicate to the other, is the degree to which spouses expect their partners to recognize and fulfill the following needs:

- *Physical:* to be physically close, to touch, to hug and be hugged, and to be sexually involved.

- *Emotional:* to feel special and important, and, conversely, to feel freedom to express their love to their partner.

- *Intellectual:* to communicate their own ideas and opinions on experiences, hopes, and dreams; together with their partner to solve problems, make plans and set goals.

- *Spiritual:* to recognize and accept the faith experience and dimension of the other, and to share common values.

As people review the story of their marriage and remember critical episodes, they may find that one or more of these needs were not being met for themselves or their partner. They also may realize that, by expecting their marriage to meet all their needs all the time, they placed an impossible burden on the relationship.

In reflecting back on their courtship and early married life, most people remember their ease in relating physically and emotionally. Early in marriage, this is often enough to keep couples happy and satisfied. However, when the glow and excitement that is part of early marriage begins to diminish, they begin to feel the need to relate on deeper intellectual and spiritual levels. If this occurs for both partners at the same time, chances are that they will grow together in love, respect and trust. If they agree on the fundamentals of how they will live—intellectually and spiritually—their union will be stable. This, of course, presupposes that they are flexible enough to allow themselves and their partners the freedom to share these vital areas of their lives with others, too.

Trouble often comes when one partner expects the other to become deeply involved in areas where it is difficult or impossible for the other to function. When one partner is not able or willing to share and communicate to the degree that the other expects, both may begin building barriers of hurt and misunderstanding between them. Their warm, positive feelings for each other slowly transform into negative ones, and they begin moving apart. With the loss of closeness, real sexual intimacy becomes increasingly difficult and their sexual relations may deteriorate.

"Moving on After Divorce; Getting Unstuck," by LeRoy Spaniol and Paul Lannan is another excellent program for those who need to focus on what one needs to do to begin to move on again. There are seven chapters in this workbook, such as, A Strategy for Getting Unstuck, The Single Life, Managing Life's Stresses, Building New Relationships, Religion and Spirituality, Sexual Affirmation, Moving on Again. The following is an excerpt from the chapter on Building New Relationships.

ATTRACTIONS AND HOOKS

Attractions are things we find pleasant and appealing in others and that others find pleasant and appealing in us. Being clear about what we like in others will increase the likelihood that we will get what we want for ourselves. At times, what we like may be out of our awareness. Or we may be embarrassed by what we like and feel that there is something wrong about liking it. (e.g., men/women with certain kinds of characteristics). What attracts us is important. When we are open to our attractions we are more likely to get into relationships that have some inherent "excitement" in them.

Hooks are things in others that feed into our deficits. If we are in a needy place emotionally we may find ourselves attracted to people who take care of our emotional needs. When our emotional needs are taken care of we may find that we have little in common with the person we are with. Anything incomplete in us can hook us in other people. In a sense, they complete us, for the moment at least. Other people cannot complete us. Relationships based on deficits are common and can even be useful during transition periods. Relationships based on strengths, mutual support and an abundance of fun have a better chance of surviving over the long haul. One of the major sources of marital breakdowns and relationship breakdowns are incomplete personal tasks which usually have very little to do with the relationship itself. Being aware of how your deficits can hook you to others and how your strengths can hook others to you is a piece of wisdom that will serve you well over the years.

EMPTY RELATIONSHIP

Sample of an Exercise—What do you find attractive in members of the opposite sex? What are some of the qualities you look for? Be specific.

Dorothy Levesque from the Diocese of Providence publishes a number of packets on a number of topics such as, Stress, Facing the Holidays, Anger, Getting to Know Me, Social Beginnings, Art of Communication. Dorothy Levesque can be contacted at the Office of Ministry with Separated, Divorced, Remarried, Widowed Persons, One Cathedral Square, Providence, Rhode Island 02903. The following is an excerpt from just one of the many packets.

COPING WITH STRESS

What Is Stress?

Webster's Seventh New Collegiate Dictionary partially defines stress as "a physical, chemical or emotional factor that causes body or mental tension and may be a factor in disease causation."

The 1978 Merriam-Webster Thesaurus uses the words "Pressure, strain, tension" as synonyms of stress.

Separated, divorced, remarried and widowed persons can't always find words to describe the stressful feelings they are experiencing; they only know they feel "overwhelmed" and feel "like they're in a pressure cooker."

Is Stress Felt Only by S.D.R.W. People?

A drastic change in life style certainly creates much stress in a person's life. However, it is important to know that EVERYONE experiences stress. It is a natural and needed part of life. Without stress, there is no growth. Consequently, stress can be growth-producing AND stress can be harmful.

What's the Difference Between the Two?

Growth-producing stress is energizing. It enables a person to stand on tiptoe to welcome life. It is the kind of stress that allows an individual to be aware of conflicting points of view or issues and seems to beckon to the individual to choose what is best for self. The important reality is that the person knows that SELF CONTROLS STRESS.

Harmful stress is confusing. It seems to turn life into a 5,000 piece puzzle—with some of the pieces missing! It is the kind of stress that seems to push the individual against the wall with no means of escape—it seems to force the individual to feel incomplete. The person seems to feel that STRESS CONTROLS SELF.

What Are Some Major Sources of Stress?

Some of the more common sources are—personal loss; change in life style; temporary internal confusion, self-imposed.

COPING WITH STRESS

Stress can also be called pressure or tension.

There will always be stress in one's life. Therefore, it is important to know that not all stress is harmful.

Living the Gospel is stressful—it puts one in conflict with the world. If a person is to be a Christian, there needs to be stress. This kind of stress is growth-producing.

Symptoms of stress appear within and without the self—in one's personal life, in relationships, in careers, etc.

SOME SOURCES OF STRESS:

1. CHANGE (internal as well as external):
   —death/divorce/remarriage certainly bring changes in one's life and are, therefore stressful;
   —each person chooses to either adjust to the change or continue to bitterly resent the change.

2. PERSONAL LOSS (especially that which is unknown to others):
   —job change/financial strain/moving/family changes;
   —each person decides for self whether the loss will be growth-producing or growth-hindering.

3. INTERNAL SOURCES OF STRESS THAT ARE TEMPORARY:
   —loss of meaning in life (why bother?);
   —aware of one's limitations (nothing I do is well done);
   —religious change and doubts (if God loves me, why does He let me experience so much pain?).

4. SELF-IMPOSED INTERNAL SOURCES OF STRESS:
   —need to be liked; fear of rejection and disapproval;
   —unrealistic expectations for self (causes guilt);

—unrealistic expectations for others (causes anger and disappointment);
—"over valuation" of own importance (can't take vacations . . . need to control);
—not accepting limitations or failures.

SOME SYMPTOMS OF STRESS:

1. Anxiety manifested by nervousness, trembling, sweating, troubled breathing, etc.
2. Depression manifested by sleeplessness or sleep disturbance, by over-eating or under-eating, etc.
3. Lower back ache, headache, nausea, etc.
4. Loss of sense of humor (NOTHING is funny).
5. Decreased sexual interest/activity.
6. Increased feelings of guilt.
7. Emotional withdrawal from friends, family, etc.
8. Increased impulsiveness, throwing self into work.
9. Increased irritibility, inappropriate reaction to situations and people.
10. Increased alcohol consumption, sexual involvement or medication.
11. Resentful of demands, every request or project becomes monumental.
12. Compulsive cleaning—or refusal to keep anything clean.
13. Inability to set limits and the inability to accept limitations—in self or others.
14. Procrastination . . . everything is put off until "later" or "tomorrow."
15. Constant questioning of one's importance.

HANDLING STRESS

Because each person is unique, there is no universal method of handling stress, each person must learn how to cope with stress in his/her own life. This list is not meant to be encyclopedic—it is meant to be of assistance as each learns his/her own method of coping.

1. Be realistic about what you can accomplish.
2. Live one day at a time.
3. Accept your limitations, set limits for yourself.
4. Re-set your goals so that they are realistic to your present lifestyle.
5. Invest in your personal growth (reading, lectures, courses, etc.)
6. Avoid unnecessary stress.
7. Keep sources of stress to a minimum—let things go!
8. Learn to accept unavoidable stress.
9. Work on internal stress factors—each person has control over his/her internal stress.
10. Learn how to profit from failure.
11. Ignore the disapproval of others.
12. Don't indulge in self-rejection.
13. Learn how to relax.
14. Take breaks/naps/vacations.
15. Eat regular, well-balanced meals.
16. Exercise (exercising the body greatly helps relieve stress).
17. Take the time to meditate—to center.

18. Breathe deeply (slowly count to 3 while inhaling; slowly count to 3 while exhaling)—
    —while inhaling, concentrate on breathing in relaxation;
    —while exhaling, concentrate on breathing out tension.

19. Learn to identify your warning signal (headache, lower back pain, feeling boxed in, etc.) and DO SOMETHING ABOUT IT!

20. "Stress is caused not only by events, but by how we view them. We can *change* our perspectives, be less hard on ourselves, accept what can't be changed. We can learn coping skills; set priorities; look for solutions to our problems, instead of automatically reaching for stress crutches—alcohol, cigarettes, food, T.V." (#20 from the January, 1982 issue of READER'S DIGEST; *Breakdown! A Journal Through Stress* by Joan Mills.)

STEPS TO WHOLENESS

SESSION I—PARTICIPANTS AGENDA—DIVORCED

I. *Theme:* DEALING WITH THE REALITY OF BEING A DIVORCED CATHOLIC TODAY.

II. *Greeting*
   Informal opening prayer
   Introduction (Members of the group pair off and share information about self with partner. Each person then introduces their partner to the group.)
   Note: Ask if it is okay to share names, addresses and phone numbers.

III. *Process:*
   1. Introduction of program, purpose, ground rules and content.
   2. Sharing:
      a. How have I been treated by family, friends, church members since my divorce?

  b. What sorts of feelings do these experiences provoke?
  c. When I say that I am a "divorced" Catholic, *how do I feel?*
  d. As a person, divorced, a Catholic, are my attitudes toward my family, friends, acquaintances and Church any different? Better or worse? How?

IV. *Closing:* Ecclesiates 3:1-15
     Song: Be Not Afraid
     Our Father (optional)

     Food for Thought: "When am I most alone?"
     (Participants prepare for next session)
     Assigned Reading: 2 Corinthians 5:13-18

V. *Handouts:* Participants Agenda
      Ground Rules
      Themes
      Bibliography

"STEPS TO WHOLENESS" published by the Arise Ministry, St. Louis, Missouri, is another structured program developed for the Separated Divorced Ministry and Widowed. Steps to Wholeness is an eight part workshop for those dealing with the divorce experience. Then there is a six part workshop for those dealing with the widowed experience. The following is an excerpt from this program. For further information contact: The Arise Ministry, 4140 Lindell Blvd., St. Louis, Missouri 63108.

STEPS TO WHOLENESS

SESSION I—PARTICIPANTS' AGENDA—WIDOWED

I. *Theme:* DEALING WITH THE REALITY OF BEING A WIDOWED CATHOLIC TODAY

II. *Greeting*
Informal prayer
Introduction (Members of the group pair off and share information about self to partner. Each person then introduces their partner to the group.)

Note: Ask if it is okay to share names, addresses and phone numbers.

III. *Process:*
1. Introduction of program, purpose, ground rules and content.
2. Input: Facilitators experience of loss.
3. Sharing:
   a. How do I feel right now?
   b. How do I feel right now about being widowed?
   c. What has been my experience so far?
   d. How do I feel about being widowed in relation to my religion?
   e. How do I feel in my own Church?
   f. Has my Church made me feel better or worse?

IV. *Closing:* Thanks
Commitment
Closing Prayer
Ecclesiastes 3:1-15
Our Father

V. *Handouts:* Participant's Agenda
Ground Rules
Themes
Bibliography

ANGER   OR EXAGGERATED?

REAL

"JOURNEY TO RECOVERY," by Jack Redman and Peggy Kenna Redman, provides a seven session program enabling participants to take giant steps toward recovery. This program includes a tape program, workbooks and facilitator's guide. For more information contact: Jack Redman and Peggy Kenna Redman, 723 W. Curry, Chandler, Ariz. 85224. The following is an excerpt from the facilitator's guide.

SUGGESTED AGENDA FOR SESSION II
SEPARATION, SHOCK & DENIAL

AGENDA	COMMENTARY	APPROX. TIME
1) Prayer (Read or spontaneous)	By facilitator/leader.	
2) Grouping by background commonalities	Such as area of U.S. where you were born (N,S,E,W) parent or no children, work outside the home or do not, etc.	20 min.
3) What did you write on Journal question, "What things do you like about yourself?"	Ask each one, write on flipchart to reinforce	10 min.
4) Informational Input "Separation, Shock, Denial"	Refer to Tape 1, Side B	15 min.
5) Awareness Exercise A	After they finish, recall analogy of bridge: ask "Have life experiences since marriage brought about changes in you, your ex-partner, that put stress on your Relationship? Share on this question in groups as set up in 2 above. Refer to P. 6, workbook.	10 min.
6) Awareness Exercise B	Do exercise alone, circle top three problem areas, share one of these top three with others in your group. Refer to P. 7 workbook.	10 min.
MIDWAY BREAK		10 min.
7) Smart Shoppers Shopping List. Reconstruct groups into all male, all female groups. From what you know now, what qualities would you want in a spouse? Write down one word descriptors on a large piece of butcher paper.	Leaders get all to participate and interject humor. When finished, each group's collage of descriptors is explained by one or two from the group—this is meant to be reflective of what they would need in a spouse for a successful relationship, yet meant to be fun too. (e.g. gentle, sexy, night person,	25 min.

"HOPE HOLDS ON" presents a program ready to go and designed to work. Joanna Dunn and Rev. Anton Braun, O.F.M. present topics covering Building Trust to Growth Beyond Divorce. The last chapter gives a basic format for dealing with almost any topic. The following is an excerpt from that chapter.

There are so many topics that can be covered and need to be covered that the list is unlimited. In our experiences we have found that the most important aspect of peer ministry is the group dynamics that is found. Rather than being concerned about having a long presentation on aa particular topic, we have found that the benefits are derived from the group for the group. People are able to learn from one another. The job of the facilitator is to keep the discussion going. When the discussion seems to die down, it is then necessary to insert a question or make a statement that will stimulate further discussion.

An example of some of the topics are: single-parenting, dealing with the ex-spouse, dating, etc. As a facilitator we recommend that you read material which pertains to the subject and be aware of current data so that you can add to the discussion whenever necessary. As a divorced person, who is a facilitator, you will be able to pull from your own experiences.

SINGLE-PARENT

The following is the format used successfully:
Materials: Newsprint or chalkboard, masking tape, felt tip markers.
Size of group: larger than 10 (format for ten or fewer follows)
Instructions: divide group into threes or fours. Have them select a spokesperson from each group. Put the word, SINGLE PARENTING, DATING, FORMER SPOUSE, etc. (whichever topic you have selected for discussion). Ask the following questions:

a) What things come to mind concerning this topic? What concerns or frustrations do you have regarding (single parenting, dating, etc.)?

b) What have been some of your experiences, both positive and negative?

You can be creative and choose other questions also. Do not restrict yourself only to our questions. We have varied them from time to time. It depends on the situation.

Once the discussion has begun, be aware of the mood of the group. You can accomplish this by moving from group to group. Once you are sure the discussion has been exhausted, then pull the group back together as a large group. Ask the spokesperson to share with the others some of the issues that emerged from the group discussions. As the spokesperson is listing these issues, write them on the newsprint or chalkboard (preferably newsprint). As you fill up one page, tape it on the wall so that it can be viewed by everyone and left up until the end of the program.

When all the groups have reported their findings, compare the similarities from each group. Encourage further discussion within the large group as time permits. This is a very successful form of getting the group involved immediately, giving them ownership.

Size of Group: (ten or fewer)—The only difference is that it is not necessary to divide the group into smaller groups. The questions can be asked of the one group and the information listed as each person responds. Encourage discussion among the group.

This is a very easy, yet most effective form of group dynamics. Try it as we have outlined first to get a feel for it, than expand it so that you are comfortable with it. This is a tool you can pull out of you "bag of tricks" at any time.

The following is another excerpts from "Hope Holds On" a chapter on Building Trust. For further information on this program contact: Alverna Center, 8140 Spring Mill Rd., Indianapolis, IN 46260.

BUILDING TRUST

In a society where the crime rate is increasing, unfaithfulness in a marriage is on the upswing, and commitment appears to be a thing of the past, it becomes much more difficult to understand and accept trust. Add all of this to the trauma of divorce and a person begins to desperately search for an opportunity to trust again.

―――――――
COMMITMENT
―――――――

When you are working with persons thrust into the crisis of separation/divorce, it is essential to always bear in mind the trust element has been almost totally erased from their lives. In a group setting, in order to establish rapport among the participants, it is necessary to rebuild this missing factor. One of the most important facts to bring out is that trust must first begin with oneself. Do you trust yourself? Your decisions? Your judgements? It is not possible to open the door to trust others if you cannot trust yourself.   **TRUST**

How do you build trust in a small group, especially if the group changes each time?

Ideally, when presenting a closed six or eight-week workshop, the facilitator is able to establish a level of trust which is easy to maintain, since the same participants remain during the entire session. When facilitating a group which changes each time, it is necessary to build to a level of trust quickly and effectively, knowing it must be repeated each session. The following are outlines for two exercises for building trust in a group.

1. Sharing in Triads or Quartets

Have the participants divide into triads, (3's) or quartets, (4's). Ask them to share on the following topics:

A. My first happiest moment that I recall.

B. My first saddest moment that I can recall.

C. A personal secret.

D. My love life, past and present.

E. If I could go back and change one day of my life, what day would that be and how would I change it?

You may use as much time as you have available for these questions. You may have them move very quickly through the questions, or have them dwell longer on one or the other.

2. Focus on Trust

Trust is the basis and foundation of growth. However, after a person has experienced the loss of trust in his/her life, there is much difficulty in restoring it again. Thus, it is of utmost importance to get in touch with the loss of trust and begin to restore it in order to build up one's life again.

Some groups develop their own program by illiciting questions from the group, that they would like discussed and thus formulate topics for the whole year.

Remember! It is important to repeat topics and programs. Here is a list of suggested topics.

- What do I do about the anger I feel?
- Why am I so angry at God?
- How do you deal with loneliness?
- What is the Churches view on divorce?
- How do I deal with depression?
- What do I do about my sexuality?
- How do I file a tax return?
- What is an annulment. How do I get one?
- How do I deal with my children?

So as you can see there are many published programs available. NACSDC has a resource center which can help you find programs.

Support Groups not only provide programs focused on personal growth but also *Spiritual Growth*. Our focus must be that of the Principles of the Catholic Church. Some ways to foster these principles are to plan spiritual activities such as:

- Weekend retreats for the Separated and Divorced
- Day of Recollection
- Parish mass especially for Separated and Divorced
- Mass prior to meeting
- Assign a Sunday mass for Separated and Divorced—sit together.
- Prayer groups
- Meditation time

Programs

- Bible study sessions
- Reflection before meetings.

Again this list can go on and on. The important thing to remember is to focus in on the principles of the Church.

SOCIAL PROGRAMS are also important since most of us have lost most of our old coupled friends. There are a few "CAUTIONS" in this area. Remember the support groups goal is to help those in the grieving process, that is where the emphasis should be. A MOTTO we use is "WORK, PLAY AND PRAYER." We must insure a balance.

The following are just suggestions, and in no way should one feel that a group should try all of these.

List of Suggested Social Functions:

- Sunday Mass followed by brunch . . .
- Pot Luck dinner . . .
- T G I F Nights . . .
- Roller skating . . .
- Movie Night (VHS—someones home)
- Square Dance
- Hay Ride
- Boat rides
- Drop-ins
- Trim a Tree Party (Christmas)
- Childrens day at the zoo
- Cooking contest (male/female)
- Camp outs

Publishing a monthly calendar can be helpful in organizing social events. One group tries to plan at least one social event a month involving children. It is also important to attend parish socials as a group.

CAUTIONS! CAUTIONS! CAUTIONS!

It's important to "pause here" just to address the area of past problems some groups have encountered.

Our groups are public meetings, from time to time people will attend support group meetings for the wrong reasons.

Every group will encounter "toxic people," those who are intensely angry, or bitter, or extremely opinionated, the know it all's, chronic complainers, blamers, waller's, instigators, drug addicts and alcohol dependent persons. One way to handle these people is to rely on your Spiritual Moderator to talk to these people and direct them toward the professional help they need.

You will also encounter what we call the "cruisers" or "social butterfly," they come to our meetings LOOKING for strictly new social experiences, prying on the vulnerability of our hurting members. Again, Leaders should make general observations at all meetings, make it a point to chat with all new members present that night, inquiring their purpose for being there. If necessary these people should be asked to leave if their motives are not in the best interest of the group. This is also true at social functions, even though it is harder to remove them from social functions.

We have also found that some members expect the group to support them financially or with housing, again this is not our responsibility we can help them by guiding them to local agencies that are set up for this purpose.

We also come across those who come, who really need professional therapy because of serious psychological problems. Again the leaders can recommend several therapists in the area or inform the Spiritual Moderator of the situation.

The next CAUTION is that of dating within the group. This can cause much hurt within the group and set many members back in the growing process. Just a word to the wise, be sensitive of others feelings. Use discretion when dating within groups. Remember there's a time and place for everything and your support group meeting is not the place to flaunt your affections for one another. It's a SUPPORT GROUP for hurting, rejected people. Again the Leaders of the group should be observant and speak to those members who violate this basic rule of sensitivity. And the last CAUTION! Publishing and circulating phone numbers of members. If members want other members to have their number they can give it to them, for obvious reasons, many already stated above. Leaders should be discreet with membership list.

V
LEADERSHIP

There are three things that every person must do in life if that person is to be successful. You must pray as though everything depends on God, Work as though everything depends on you and play as though you really enjoy life.

I would first like to share with you from "Hope Holds On" what leadership is.

"Leadership is a process of facilitating the goal achievement of an individual or of a group in a particular situation. Because leadership is human, even in a church community, it must deal with the complexity of human beings. The leader needs to know himself or herself, his or her needs and motives; he or she needs to know the assumptions that he or she makes about people, because these will show in his or her behavior; he or she needs to recognize the fallibility of his or her perceptions, when to trust them and what to question them; he or she needs to know the situation into which he or she will channel his or her leadership functions and train others to do the same. Most of all, if he or she chooses or is chosen to lead, he or she needs to serve."

"A CALL TO LEADERSHIP IS A CALL TO MINISTRY"

Below are some qualities to consider when looking for leaders.

1. An ability to take feedback—know that your ideas are not the only ones and listening to feedback and accepting feedback is very important. A sign of growth.

2. An ability to risk—realization of humanity—leaders can make mistakes—confident and willing to trust enough to risk.

3. Show initiative—able to begin and follow through with a task.

4. Positive self concept—"I may not be perfect, but I know I can do this."

5. An ability to trust others—letting go—delegating tasks—Attitude that others can do just as good if not better than me. Not, "No one can do it like I can."

6. Accepting responsibility—whether right or wrong.

7. Commitment—ability to be involved—become an active participant, not just talk.

8. An ability to reach out to others when in need of support.

9. The ability to see the potential in others. Some insight.

10. An ability to be objective. To see both sides of an issue.

11. An ability to listen—this has been stressed over and over. Hear what others are telling you.

12. An ability to be flexible. "BENDABLE" "go with the flow."

13. Openness—Ability to be open to new ideas—an awareness and ability to allow change.

14. An ability to be sensitive—gentle—patient.

15. An ability to challenge—allows others to grow.

16. An ability to encourage others—approving.

17. An ability to compromise—for the good of the group.

Before we go any further there seems to be a need, at least on my part, to clarify a few terms. The word "Leader" conotes to me someone in control. Maybe it would be better to change the word "Leader" to "Ministers to the Grieving." Dorothy Levesque stresses this concept of "minister" or "ministry aides," which I will address shortly. There also seems some need to clarify the difference between "Group Leaders" and "Facilitators."

Leadership

"Group Leader," "Core Group Leader," "Group Coordinator" in my understanding are those individuals who are far enough along their own "growing process" to be able to assume some responsibility for the group. This could be only in the area of organizing and structure. This person may also be very well qualified to act as facilitator. The "facilitator" may not have any organizational responsibilities except for facilitating a group in group discussion. So when we speak of developing leadership it's important to look at all these roles.

You may have a member who is very organized, very tuned into detail, is good at follow through. This person may very well be just the person to run the meetings as a group coordinator.

Then there may be that member who is a very good listener, very sensitive to peoples feelings and you feel this sense of "spirit" this might just be the facilitator you've been looking for the newcomers group.

So when we say develop leadership it is more than just someone who can organize a meeting. Look for the talents within your group, it's there! It might be fun and interesting to have a meeting where everyone list their own strengths and also the kinds of things they like to do. Gathering that data will give many insights.

Basically what we are asking people to do when we ask them to become leaders is to "walk with" others who are experiencing the same pain they experienced. Share your journey.

A training period needs to be provided for those who are willing to make a commitment. Dorothy Levesque uses a "three phase" approach. All potential leaders are asked this question. Should I take this leadership training? Answer yes, if, "I have experienced a very deep loss in my life and have the courage to deal with the loss." If one answers, "I am here to help others," this does not meet the criteria. In order to become a leader you first must understand the concept of "walking with, minister with them."

Phase I contains four two-hour sessions. The first session takes participants through the phases of the grieving process. The writings of Elisabeth Kubler-Ross are the foundation of this presentation.

Support Group leaders need to understand that support groups allow an "Emotional Rest Period." Just as Christ invites us all to "Come to me all you are labored and are heavy burdened I will give you rest." The support group is a place where one is ALLOWED to express anger or any other feeling. And leaders need to have a clear understanding of this concept.

The second session of Phase I is spent on Programs of Ministry, such as, How to facilitate groups, Retreat programs, P R work, How to select presentors of programs. The third session deals with facilitation skills, listening skills, ground rules for group discussion. The following are five rules or ground rules for groups.

- CONFIDENTIALITY
- ONE PERSON SPEAKS AT A TIME
- ALLOWED TO BE SILENT
- NO ONE GIVES ADVICE ONLY SHARING IDEAS
- CONSCIENTIOUS OF TIME EQUAL TIMES FOR ALL PARTICIPANTS

The fourth session is spent on public relations and any questions regarding prior sessions.

At this point in the training, participants can drop out and not proceed to Phase II.

Phase II consist of nine monthly meetings, these meetings are all designed to feed leaders. What are other leaders doing? What is working or not working? This phase is a way of nurturing leaders. (Who need it also.)

At the end of Phase II leaders have participated in 25 hours of training. At this time they are presented a certificate of completion and asked to make a two year commitment.

That is only one approach to leadership training. Dorothy Levesque has found this approach very successful and that is after seven years of experience. If anyone is interested in this program you can contact Dorothy Levesque.

SHORT COURSE IN HUMAN RELATION COMMUNICATION

The **SIX** most important words ...."I ADMIT I MADE A MISTAKE"
The **FIVE** most important words................................"YOU DID A GOOD JOB"
The **FOUR** most important words..........................."WHAT IS YOUR OPINION"

Leadership

The **THREE** most important words ...."IF YOU PLEASE"
The **TWO** most important words ...."THANK YOU"
The **ONE** most important word.."WE"
The **LEAST** important words ...."I" or "MY"

FACILITATOR

The facilitator is the one who "makes things easier, or less difficult," at least that's how it's defined in the dictionary.

Within our groups the facilitator enables the group to function. How, by making physical arrangements, opening and closing meetings, keeping discussion on track and on going, being sensitive, listening and watching. We must remember facilitators are not expected to be a teacher, counselor or therapist. It is the members' responsibility to help each other learn and heal. The facilitators are responsible in helping to provide the climate where this can take place.

Facilitators who have experienced divorce will have a deeper insight and compassion for those working through the initial crisis. But a word of caution to facilitators. Facilitators should be careful not to allow any personal hangups resulting from their own divorce to influence the discussions. Must beware of our natural tendency to be judgmental.

DEEPER INSIGHT

COMPASSION

The following are several areas facilitators should be aware of:

1. Remember! try not to fall into the role of "Rescuer." You can *not* solve problems, you *can* listen and respect the feelings that are being expressed.

2. Body language—you may give the impression of not being accepting if, for instance, you stand in front of a group with your arms tightly crossed or turning your shoulders away from the group. You may give the impression of being bored or not interested in them if you sit there tapping your fingers or pencil. So be aware of your body language.

3. Avoid coming to a meeting with a preconceived plan of what should happen. Yes, you must plan for each session but, you are there as the facilitator.

4. "Bite your tongue." The group is where most people try to deal with their negative feelings. Sometimes you may feel troubled by what is said. All feelings are real and should be acknowledged and accepted. We are trying to help deal with these negative emotions in a positive way.

5. You may experience from time to time that the group will digress from the topic. Some decision making needs to take place as allowing the digression or pulling them back to the topic. If the topic captures the interest of the group it is perfectly O.K. to allow discussion to continue. Remember facilitators open discussion and should feel it's O K to be flexible. There's no rigid schedules.

6. Remember! You will make mistakes. It has been proven that most of the members of a group are caring people. They will accept their own. RELAX!, DON'T GET UPTIGHT!.

The following are several guidelines for Group Facilitators.

1. Facilitator facilitates rather than leads. Helps the members of the group develop and express their thoughts, not the facilitator's thoughts.

2. Facilitators try to develop a trust level in the group so that each person feels at ease and knows his/her contributions will be valued.

3. Facilitators risk open communication of his/her own feelings and thoughts when appropriate.

4. Facilitators try to be sensitive to the needs of each person, watching for signs of uneasiness, boredom, hurt feelings, etc.

5. Facilitators try to insure that one or two people don't monopolize the discussion. Also must guard against monopolizing it with self.

6. Facilitators try to draw each person into the discussion, but without putting anyone on the spot or being "threatening."

7. Facilitators do not assume he/she knows what group members think but continually tries to draw out their feelings, thoughts and reactions.

8. Facilitators try to help people get in touch with their feelings and express them within the group.

9. Facilitators try to facilitate as a "team" with partner.

10. Facilitators try to get discussion started, keep it going, and concludes it at the proper time.

Leadership

11. Facilitators do not feel uncomfortable by lack of responses to questions asked, or lack of knowledge on the part of group members, or periods of silence within the group, and do not feel pressured to fill these gaps by talking about self.

12. To help start discussion a leadoff question should be used. This is a question that can't be answered by "yes" or "no" statements. For example: How does this topic relate to your own personal experience?

13. Allow for periods of silence. Members need time to think. You may want to try to rephrase the question.

14. Try to get others to speak. This sometimes needs a Pull-in question. For example: Does anyone else have a comment?

15. Try using "I" statements. For example: "I imagine you are feeling very angry right now."

VI

HOW TO PUBLICIZE YOUR GROUP

It is easy to give advice—it is harder to take advice—but without advice and help we will not grow in the practice of life.

- MEANS OF PUBLICITY:

    RADIO
    T.V.
    BULLETIN BOARDS
    (supermarkets, Post Office, Library)
    NEWSPAPER
    FLYERS
    NEWSLETTERS
    PERSONAL CONTACT
    TELEPHONE
    CHURCH BULLETIN

- HOW TO GET NOTICED:

    YOUR PRESS RELEASE OR FLYER MUST BE CONCISE.
    IT SHOULD BE COMPACT. That means it can't be to WORDY.
    IT SHOULD BE CATCHY.
    IT SHOULD BE CURRENT.
    YOU CAN'T OVERLOAD A PAGE.
    IT HAS TO BE NEAT.

Sometimes it's helpful to contact the media to find out what their CRITERIA is. What their DEADLINES are. What their SPECIFICATIONS are.

As far as SDRC is concerned you must understand your own needs. Your audience, your geographical area, your criteria. For example, are you trying to reach hurting people or trying to get more numbers to your groups.

BEFORE YOU WRITE TO SOURCES

- give them (newspaper, local radio) a call and get the correct name of the person or section that will be handling this.
- make sure you get their DEADLINE.
- use a LONG envelop to send your publicity in. (Small ones somehow get lost.)
- LOWER right hand corner should have the name or section that your article is going to.
- send to THREE key persons. One to general newspaper editor, one to Religion news editor, one to Area Happenings editor or Social column editor. Your chances of having one of the three pick up your article is more likely.
- our local Pennysaver request POST CARDS. Use LARGE SIZE post cards. Using COLORED ones has also proved successful.

WHEN DO YOU WANT THIS PUBLICIZED?

It's important to remember that it is the medias' time that is important not yours. Make sure you know their deadlines and stick to it. This information can be obtained through a simple phone call.

Know the day you want it published. For example, if your meeting is on Tuesday, you would want to get the information out to the public by the previous Friday. This allows sufficient time for people to make babysitting arrangements etc.

SUGGEST that it be published on a certain day, NEVER TELL THEM.

How to Publicize Your Group

Indicate this date in RED. Always give an alternative date. For example: Would you be so kind to publish this on Wednesday September 12, or Thursday, September 13th.

Always end by saying "Thank You for your help." Again use RED pen.

The following are some sample forms of the ENVELOP and NEWS RELEASE:

FIVE points that are most important in writing any news release.

1. WHO
2. WHAT
3. WHERE
4. WHEN
5. HOW

We have found that RADIO usually want a three by five card. It's important to remember to give each media what they want. Colored post cards catch the eye. Color inks catch the eye. Underlining catch the eye.

Here is a sample of a smaller post card:

SEPARATED, DIVORCED, REMARRIED CATHOLICS
GRAYMOOR, GARRISON, N.Y.
PHONE (914) 424-3671

SUGGESTED DATES
OCT. 15, 16, 17

Rev. William Murphy, a national authority on separated people, will lecture on the Catholic Church's views on divorce at St. John's Church, Route 6, Beacon, N.Y. on Tuesday, Oct. 21 at 8:00 p.m. If you are lonely, bitter, or filled with guilt come and learn how to become a whole person and live to be happy once again.

Diana Oddo
(914) 628-5302

VII
RESOURCES

An optimist is a person who looks at a glass and it is half full
A pessimist is a person who looks at a glass and it is half empty

There are a variety of resources which are useful to Catholics who are separated, divorced or remarried. We list a few we have discovered in the following pages, in no particular order. As your group develops, you will find other resources. Please share them with others running support groups.

SEPARATED, DIVORCED & REMARRIED CATHOLICS

DISCUSSION TOPICS FOR MINI-GROUPS

LONELINESS
1. Is it a problem?
2. Aloneness and loneliness—Which do you have? How do you deal with it?

GUILT AND ANGER
1. How do you deal with your own feelings of anger and guilt toward yourself, when you are, at the same time, feeling anger and resentment toward your spouse?
2. How do you handle developments of resentment and bitterness?
3. How do you get over the feeling of guilt, especially as far as the children are concerned?
4. Introduction to Assertiveness Training—Discuss the "Bill of Assertive Rights" as found in the book by Manual J. Smith—"What I Say No, I Feel Guilty."

RELIGION AND SPIRITUALITY
1. As SDRC members, what obligations do we have to each other?
2. How did your divorce affect your relations with your Church and Priest?
3. Why do I come to SDRC? What are some things we can do for new members and for each other, to be more supportive?
4. At Thanksgiving time—What do I have to be thankful for?

SPIRITUAL/RELIGIOUS TOPICS WITH A SPIRITUAL MODERATOR PRESENT
(Priest or Sister)
1. Remarriage without an annulment.
2. Church teaching versus individual conscience.
3. Faith—the positive plus in your future.
4. General absolution without individual confession.
5. Being away from church and religious experiences, and how to get involved again.
6. Does God really listen and does He care?
7. Peace of mind through the Church.
8. Question and answer period on any aspect of our Catholic faith.

TRUSTING
1. After you cope with divorce and enter into a new relationship and build trust, what happens when that falls apart?
2. Trusting self and others—Again, or perhaps for the first time.

PROBLEMS
1. Rejection by friends.
2. Confronting friends, relatives; co-workers who are not aware of your situation.
3. Negative reactions of relatives towards your separation and divorce.
4. Acceptance by the community.
5. Have you had problems with your parents not being able to accept your divorce?
6. How do you deal with a situation which makes it necessary to be in the company of your ex-spouse and his/her new partner?

Resources

7. If your children are young, under 8 years old when you divorce, do you feel the trauma they experience is lessened? Will the problems come later in life?

EMOTIONS

1. How many "tunnels" does one have to go through? How do you handle the variety of emotions.
2. Letting go—of what—how?
3. What is love? I thought I knew what love was when I married. I don't love myself. Am I too selfish to love?
4. Where do you want to go from here?
5. How am I coping? What was the week like?

HOW DO YOU HANDLE AND/OR GET RID OF:

1. Loneliness.
2. Self pity.
3. Anger.
4. Bitterness.
5. High and low periods.

BEING SINGLE, DATING AND NEW RELATIONSHIPS

1. Improving your social life.
2. Dating again—When is it O.K.
3. How do we deal with new relationships? When do you introduce children to "someone new." How can we help our children accept our new relationships?
4. Starting over—The singles scene.
5. How can I help myself to remain safely unemotionally involved when dating? What are some hints?
6. Would you get married again?
7. Will I be able to adapt to a new relationship after being alone?
8. Second relationships.
9. Views on marriage. A. older man/younger woman. B. The reverse.

FAMILY

1. How do you explain to the children that Mommy and Daddy have to start forming a new life for his or her self?
2. Dealing with teenagers.
3. Should you give up your life to devote to your children?
4. Should the weekend parent punish the child when the ex has informed him the child was bad.
5. Communicating with your children—The right word at the right time.
6. Relating to your former spouse or former in-laws.

CHILDREN AND/OR PARENTS

Children and their thoughts towards:

1. Their marrying.
2. Your remarrying.
3. Your dating.
4. Their feelings before, during and after the break-up.

HOW DO YOU HANDLE:

1. Birthdays.
2. Graduations.
3. Thanksgiving.
4. Christmas, etc.
5. Vacations.

Handling childrens' anger and your own guilt. Your and the childrens' reaction when the divorce becomes final.

STRUGGLE BETWEEN PARENT AND CHILDREN IN ONE PARENT HOUSEHOLD

1. Discipline.
2. Rules.
3. Behavior.
4. School, etc.

How to approach the wedding of your children. Who gets invited (mother/father)? Who sits where, etc.

LAWYERS AND LEGAL SITUATIONS

1. Legal aspects of separation and divorce. (Have a lawyer present)
   A. Taxes   B. Real Estate   C. Wills and Estates
2. What do you like and/or dislike about your lawyer. How can you form a more comfortable relationship.

ANNULMENTS

1. How do you feel about the Church's view? Is it really the Church's way of accepting divorce.
2. Explain how this would affect children. Is it really necessary.

HEALING

1. You know you are healed when you can accept your share of the responsibility for the ending of your marriage. React and discuss this.
2. Letting go and moving on—going beyond divorce.
3. What is being good to yourself?
4. How did I contribute to the break-up of my marriage? Could I make a better marriage partner now?
5. How do you develop contentment and self-confidence.
6. How do you manage to get a high self-esteem and go about keeping it.

MONEY, FINANCES AND BUDGETS

1. Selling a house.
2. Property distribution.
3. Moving
4. Renting vs. holding onto house.
5. Investment
6. Taxes—Alimony, child support and dependents.
7. Legal rights.

Resources 77

8. College costs—Scholarships, federal & state funds, TAP
9. What can be done to get SDRC cards to carry for discounts, etc.

SEXUALITY

My Sexuality. Do I have it? What do I do with it?

1. How do I handle close contact with the opposite sex? Am I ready?
2. Can there be sex without involvement?
3. When will I be ready? Am I ready now?
4. Is sex a commitment?
5. Must I be in love?
6. With whom do I get involved?
7. Should I feel guilty? Is it right not to feel guilty?
8. If I have children, how does this affect my relationship with them?
9. Is it a sin to have sex and not be married?

MISCELLANEOUS TOPICS

1. Men's panel. Sharing their experiences. The other side of the fence.
2. What are the community resources available to the single parent.

IF I HAD TO DO IT OVER AGAIN

IF I HAD TO DO IT OVER AGAIN, I'd try
to make more mistakes next time,
    I would relax a little more.
        I would limber up quite a bit,
      and be a little sillier than I
        have been this trip.

I know there would be very few things
I would take so seriously,
    and I would be crazier,
    and certainly less hygienic.

I'd take more chances, I'd take more
non-sense journeys.
    I would climb more mountains and
      swim more rivers and
      watch more sunsets . . .
    I'd fuss less about myself, and
      think a little more of the
      value of myself . . .
    I'd burn a great deal more
      gasoline.

I'd eat more ice-cream and less beans.
    I'd have more actual troubles and
    fewer imaginary ones.
      You see, I'm one of those
      people who is highly organized
        Very sane and sensible,
          and that's why I live
            hour after hour
            and day after day.

Oh, I have had my moments . . .
    And if I had to do it over again, I'd
    have more of them!

In fact, that's what I'd have
most of . . . just moments . . .
one after another, instead of
this living so many years
ahead of each day.

I have been one of those people who
never go anywhere without a
    thermometer, a raincoat,
    second this or that.
But if I had to do it over again,
    I would go more places.
I'd get up and go quickly and travel
    much lighter than I ever have
    and I would go places
    I never dream I'd go.

If I had my life to live again,
    I'd start barefooted earlier
    in the spring
    and I would stay that way
    until later in the fall.

I would play hockey more, and I wouldn't
    make such good grades either . . .
    except by accident

I would ride more merry-go-rounds.

AND I'D CERTAINLY PICK MORE DAISIES!

Author unknown

FORMING A CONSCIENCE

1. TAKE THE TIME
   —conscious effort to set time aside for reflection, etc.
   —be aware that conscience formation is a process.

2. CREATE THE SPACE
   —not enough to take time—must also clear the "inner space" to allow room for conscience formation information.

3. NO FAST SOLUTION
   —real life isn't a situation comedy that can be resolved in one hour.
   —accept the fact that the process takes time.

4. CHILD'S CONSCIENCE FORMATION
   —imitation (follow the leader; be one of the crowd)
   —fear (if I don't do good, I'll be punished)
   —guilt feelings (if I don't do good and something bad happens to someone I love, it will be MY fault)
   —compulsion (seems like the right thing to do at the moment).

5. ADULT'S CONSCIENCE FORMATION
   —conviction (I know this is good for me)
   —freedom (no one is forcing me to do this)
   —choice (of all the alternatives, I choose this one)
   —decision (this is my decision, I won't change my mind in 10 minutes).

6. TEACHING
   —what does today's Church teach?
   —what did Jesus teach about this?

7. OPTIONS
   —there is never just one way to do anything
   —what alternatives are there?
   —being aware of alternatives often removes a "being pushed in the corner" feeling.

8. DISCUSS
   —speak with people you trust and whose opinion you respect
   —speak with people who have had a similar decision to make
   —speak with people who are knowledgeable.

9. PRAY
   —speak with God
   —be confident that He WILL help you.

10. LISTEN
    —it isn't enough to speak to people, you must also LISTEN to the response
    —it isn't enough to speak to God, you must also BE STILL and let Him be God for you.

11. BE OPEN TO GOD
    —don't limit God's power within you
    —fear often closes a person's openness to God
    —let Him explode His knowledge within you.

Resources

12. BE TRUE TO YOURSELF
    —other people should not be the reason you make a decision
    —be honest with yourself.
13. BE INFORMED
    —read, listen, talk with others, pray!
14. BE AWARE OF YOUR INNER VOICE
    —possible only if you take the time and create the space
    —"Be still and know that I am God"
    —trust yourself.
15. —be gentle with yourself.
    —we are constantly forming our consciences; as we grow as persons, our horizons are broadened
    —what was right for me last year may not be right for me today
    —what is right for me today may not be right for me next year
    —be gentle with yourself!

FACING THE HOLIDAYS

1. CHOICE
   —Dwell on past
   —Fantasize future
   —Live in present
2. CRY AND SHARE PAIN
3. REST
   —Save your energy
4. BE WITH PEOPLE WHO LOVE YOU
5. DO WHAT IS GOOD FOR YOU
6. ACCEPT: IT *IS* DIFFERENT NOW
7. CREAT NEW TRADITIONS
8. DO (OR BUY) SOMETHING SPECIAL FOR YOU
9. BE GENTLE WITH YOURSELF
10. KNOW: GOD LOVES YOU
11. FIRST CHRISTMAS
    —Jesus, Mary, Joseph
    —Poor and homeless
12. CENTER ON GOD
13. THANKSGIVING
    —Thank God for being God
14. CHRISTMAS
    —Adore God for becoming human
15. NEW YEAR
    —Engage God for the coming year
16. YES
17. CHILDREN *NEED*
    —gentle love
    —express feelings
    —honesty
    —understanding
    —quiet time
    —know meaning of day

DEALING WITH EMOTIONS: CHILDREN

1. DEATH/DIVORCE
   —Traumatic experience even when anticipated
   —Causes drastic change in life style
   —Creates rash of emotions

2. SHOCK
   —Numb
   —Can't feel anything
   —Often function like a robot
   —Doesn't seem to be reacting
   —System unable to accept full impact

3. DENIAL
   —Inability to accept the reality of divorce or death
   —Often fantasize activities and conversations with the absent parent
   —Make up stories with friends

4. BARGAINING
   —Wants to make a deal
   —Will do anything to get things back as they were/back to normal
   —Will try to become a matchmaker with divorced parents/won't let dead parent's things be given or thrown away

5. ANGER
   —Resents fact that family has been turned upside down
   —Resents fact that there's only "half of a family"
   —Resents being embarrassed at father/daughter dance, etc.

6. FEAR
   —Afraid of being left alone
   —Afraid parent (at home) won't be able to carry burden
   —Afraid that college/career plans will have to change
   —Afraid that friends' families will reject him/her

7. GUILT
   —Assumes responsibility for the death/divorce
   —"If I had (or) hadn't . . ."
   —"I *should* have (or) *shouldn't* have . . ."
   —Carries the burden of having caused the death or divorce

8. REJECTION
   —The absent parent doesn't seem to care
   —"I'm not wanted even by the people who are supposed to care most"
   —Friends don't know how to react and often leave the person alone—and thus intensify feeling of rejection

9. HATRED
   —Hatred of absent parent (for deserting me)
   —Hatred of present parent

10. INSECURITY
    —Everything is different
    —Not sure about money
    —Not sure about living in same house
    —Afraid of what others are thinking

11. DEPRESSION
    —Loses all ambition
    —Loses all interest in friends, activities, school work and/or job
    —Doesn't seem to care about personal appearance
    —Seems to "give up"

12. LONELINESS
    —Feels alone/abandoned

Footprints in the Sand...

One night a man had a dream. He dreamed he was walking along the beach with the LORD. Across the sky flashed scenes from his life. For each scene, he noticed two sets of footprints in the sand; one belonging to him, and the other to the LORD.

When the last scene of his life flashed before him, he looked back at the footprints in the sand. He noticed that many times along the path of his life there was only one set of footprints. He also noticed that it happened at the very lowest and saddest times in his life.

This really bothered him and he questioned the LORD about it. "LORD, you said that once I decided to follow you, you'd walk with me all the way. But I have noticed that during the most troublesome times in my life, there is only one set of footprints. I don't understand why when I needed you most you would leave me."

The LORD replied, "My precious, precious child, I love you and I would never leave you. During your times of trial and suffering, when you see only one set of footprints, it was then that I carried you."

Author unknown

ALL BY MYSELF

O God, I'm alone, It's hard to feel that anyone cares, including you, O God.
I wonder if anyone understands my wanting a friend who don't want nothing from me.
Help me to believe you are my friend and to know you are with me.
Keep me from making a fool of myself.
I don't want to become bitter and filled with hate—I've seen too much hate.
I don't want to be angry anymore.
Forgive me, please. For what I have done, and help me live right again.
I pray, wondering if you hear me.

Carl Burke

One day a man saw a butterfly, shuddering on the sidewalk,
locked in a seemingly hopeless struggle
to free itself from its now—useless cocoon.
Feeling pity, he took a pocket knife,
carefully cut away the cocoon and set the butterfly free.
To his dismay, it lay on the sidewalk,
convulsed weakly for a while, and died,
A biologist later told him,
"that was the worst thing you could have done!
A butterfly needs that struggle to
develop the muscles to fly.
By robbing him of the struggle,
you made him too weak to live."

Author unknown

'I HAVE MY MISSION'

God has created me to do Him some definite service;
   He has committed some work to me which He has not committed to
      another.
I have my mission . . .

I am a link in a chain,
   a bond of connection between persons.
      He has not created me for naught.
         I shall do good.
            I shall do His work.
I shall be an angel of peace,
   a preacher of truth in my own place
      while not intending it—
         if I do but keep His commandments.
Therefore I will trust Him.

Whatever, wherever I am, I can never be thrown away.
   If I am in sickness, my sickness may serve Him;
      in perplexity, my perplexity may serve Him;
         if I am in sorrow, my sorrow may serve Him.
He does nothing in vain.
        He knows what He is about.

                        (John Henry Cardinal Newman)

You were born to serve a purpose.

    This purpose is what we call your "mission,"
                your reason for being,
                        your Earth—trip.
To find this out is a trip in itself
                      but it is all a part of growth.
In order to accomplish your true life's work,
      you must first establish the path by which you are
                                to reach it.
Everything in life is a step toward or a vehicle to reach something higher.

                                    (Alan Oken)

PERSONS ARE GIFTS At least Jesus thought so: "Father, I want those you have *given* me to be where I am . . ." I agree with Jesus . . . and I also want those whom the Father has given me to be where I am!

Persons are gifts which the Father sends to me . . . wrapped!

Some are wrapped very beautifully; they are attractive when I first see them.
Some come in very ordinary wrapping paper.
Others have been mishandled in the mail.
Once in a while there is a "special delivery!"
Some persons are gifts which come very loosely wrapped.
   Others vary tightly.

But the wrapping is not the gift!
It is so easy to make this mistake . . . it's amusing when babies do it.
Sometimes the gift is very easy to open up.
Sometimes I need others to help. Is it because they are afraid?
        Does it hurt?
        Maybe they have been opened up before . . . and . . .
            thrown away!

I am a person. Therefore, I am a gift too!
A gift to myself, first of all. The Father gave myself to me.
Have I ever really looked inside the wrappings? Afraid to?

Perhaps I've never accepted the gift I am . . .
Could it be that there is something else inside the wrappings than what
I think there is?
Maybe I've never seen the wonderful gift that I am!
Could the Father's gift be anything but beautiful?
I love the gifts which those who love me give to me . . . why not this gift from the
                Father?
Am I a gift to other persons?
   Am I willing to be given by the Father to others? . . . A person for others?
   Do others have to be content with the wrappings . . .
                never permitted to enjoy the
                gifts?

Every meeting of persons is an exchange of gifts.
But a gift without a giver is not a gift; it is a thing devoid of a relationship
to a giver or givee.

Friendship is a relationship between persons who see themselves as they truly are:
        gifts of the Father to each other for others . . .
        brothers and sisters.

A friend is a gift not just to me but to others through me.
   When I keep my friend . . . possess my friend . . . I destroy my friend. GIFT-NESS!
   If I save his life for me, I lose it; if I lose it for others, I save it.

Persons are gifts, gifts received and gifts given . . . like the Son.
   Friendship is the response of person-gifts to the Father-giver.
   Friendship is *Eucharist!* Friendship is JOY! Friendship is YOU!

Author unknown